Bee
KIND
to
YOURSELF
And Don't Forget to Fill Your Honey Jar

By Corey Anne Abreau | Edited by Sara Letourneau

There are a few things to keep in mind:
Always be grateful, loving, and kind,
Not only to yourself, but to others, too.
Kindness begins with taking care of you.

By ensuring your honey jar is filled every day,
You'll help keep those not-so-pleasant moments at bay.
Eat, drink, laugh, sleep, and play.
Take care of you, and everything will be okay.

Look in the mirror; I bet you'll agree.
You are as important as can be.

There will be times when you'll be on your way,
And you'll have the most magical day,

Feeling happy, excited, maybe even proud,
Or relaxed and calm, as if floating on a cloud.

Enjoy these good days, and take it all in,
And know that your happiness comes from within.

Occasionally, you may feel sad,
Tired, bored, or even mad.
Any fear or anger may come and go.
As you learn to manage your emotions, you will grow.

Oftentimes, crying can be a helpful release.
Afterward, you will likely feel a sense of peace.

When those stormy days come, don't shy away.
Be extra kind to yourself that day.

Take a nap in your warm, cozy bed.
Or choose a favorite book to read instead.
Say positive affirmations out loud.
Believe in those words, and also be proud.

I AM AMAZING
I AM BEAUTIFUL
IAM CARING

It is so important to practice self-care.
Take a stroll outside for some nice fresh air.
Relax your body, and breathe in self-love.
Exhale the emotions you want to let go of.

As much as you can, fill up your honey jar.
It will make you feel wonderful wherever you are.
It will always be much simpler to find
The best ways to be grateful, loving, and kind,

Not only to yourself, but to others, too.
Remember, kindness begins with taking care of you.

HOW ARE YOU *feeling* TODAY?

BEE KIND TO YOURSELF

HAPPY	SAD	ANGRY

PROUD

CONFUSED

SILLY

CALM

TIRED

SICK

SHY

NERVOUS
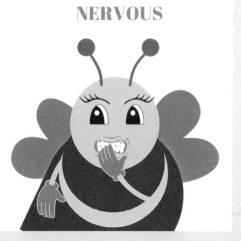

FRUSTRATED

MY PLAN
TO FILL MY HONEY JAR

• • • • • • • • • • • • • • • • • • •

Exercising and eating healthy

• • • • • • • • • • • • • • • • • • •

Write in my journal

• • • • • • • • • • • • • • • • • • •

List what I am grateful for

• • • • • • • • • • • • • • • • • • •

Offer a helping hand

• • • • • • • • • • • • • • • • • • •

Say positive affirmations

• • • • • • • • • • • • • • • • • • •

Take a swim in the pool

• • • • • • • • • • • • • • • • • • •

I WILL CONTINUE TO BEE AMAZING

MY PLAN
TO FILL MY HONEY JAR

• •

• •

• •

• •

• •

• •

• •

I WILL CONTINUE TO BEE AMAZING

TODAY I FEEL

Emotions Cards

DISAPPOINTED

ANGRY

FRUSTURATED

CONFUSED

WORRIED

SILLY

NERVOUS

HAPPY

CALM

PROUD

EXCITED

TIRED

SICK

SAD

BORED

TODAY I FEEL

HOW CAN I FEEL BETTER?

WHEN YOU FEEL ... YOU CAN

GREAT
• • • • • • • • • •

YOU ARE DOING UN-BEE-LIEVABLE
CONTINUE PRACTICING SELF-CARE

GOOD
• • • • • • • • • •

GOOD JOB - **KEEP** BEE-**ING AMAZING**
TRY TO STAY WHERE YOU ARE

OKAY
• • • • • • • • • •

BEE KIND TO YOURSELF - DO YOU NEED REST? FOOD? HUGS?
DO SOMETHING YOU ENJOY TO MAKE THE DAY BETTER

BLAH
• • • • • • • • • •

TRY BEE-**ING KINDER TO YOURSELF** - WHAT IS BOTHERING
YOU? WHAT DO YOU NEED RIGHT NOW?
Food / Sleep / Love / Exercise

DRAINED
• • • • • • • • • •

TAKE ACTION AND PRACTICE YOUR COPING SKILLS
SO YOU CAN GET BACK TO FEELING
UN-BEE-LIEVABLE

COPING SKILLS

HOW TO FILL UP YOUR HONEY JAR

- Deep breathing exercises.
- Repeat your positive affirmations out loud.
- Relax your body and mind by meditating and resting.
- Do some journaling, writing or drawing.
- Go for a run or a walk outside.
- Dance, jump, or skip. Maybe listen to music while you do this.
- Sit down with a friend or family member in a calming corner, and talk about what is bothering you.
- Read a good book.
- Watch a funny movie.
- Play a musical instrument.
- Do arts and crafts.
- Eat healthy foods, and drink lots of water.
- Remember, it's okay to not be okay. Ask for help if things don't get better after you use your coping skills.

YOU ARE UN-BEE-LIEVABLE

CHECK YOUR HONEY JAR

I FEEL GREAT
YOU ARE DOING UN-**BEE**-LIEVABLE
CONTINUE PRACTICING SELF-CARE

I FEEL GOOD
GOOD JOB - **KEEP BEE-ING AMAZING**
TRY TO STAY WHERE YOU ARE

I FEEL OKAY
BEE KIND TO YOURSELF - DO YOU NEED REST? FOOD? HUGS?
DO SOMETHING YOU ENJOY TO MAKE THE DAY BETTER

I FEEL BLAH
TRY BEE-ING KINDER TO YOURSELF - WHAT IS BOTHERING YOU?
WHAT DO YOU NEED RIGHT NOW? Food / Sleep / Love / Exercise

I FEEL DRAINED
TAKE ACTION AND PRACTICE YOUR COPING SKILLS
SO YOU CAN GET BACK TO FEELING UN-**BEE**-LIEVABLE

HONEY JAR

WRITE OUT & COLOR IN HOW YOU ARE FEELING

I FEEL GREAT

I FEEL GOOD

I FEEL OKAY

I FEEL BLAH

I FEEL DRAINED

Made in United States
Troutdale, OR
04/09/2024

19048754R00021